Simply Breads
& Accompaniments

Quick & Easy Indian
Simply Breads
& Accompaniments

Lustre Press
Roli Books

All rights reserved. No part of this publication may be
transmitted or reproduced in any form or by any means
without prior permission of the publisher.

ISBN: 978-81-7436-822-5

For the recipes we are grateful to Bina Parasramka, Jeani
Mohindra, Kalp Mithal, Loke Rajye Laxmi Devi, Prima
Kurien, Pushpesh Pant, and Vijaylakshmi Baig.

Photographs: Sunny Singh, Dheeraj Paul

© Roli & Janssen/Roli Books 2011
Published in India by Roli Books
in arrangement with Roli & Jansen BV
M 75 Greater Kailash II (Market),
New Delhi 110 048, India.
Phone: ++91-11-29212271, 40682000.
Fax: ++91-1129217185
Email: info@rolibooks.com
Website: www.rolibooks.com

Editor: Neeta Datta
Design: Supriya Saran
Prepress: Jyoti Dey

Printed and bound in China

Contents

Introduction

B read is integral to the dining culture of India. It is generally referred to as roti in the local language. The growth of a wide range of cereals and grains in the country has led to the preparation of different types of breads. Each differs from the other in the ingredients used, in the shape, size, and the taste. The cooking method too differs widely from one part of the country to another. The Indian bread is generally composed of flour made of wheat, rice, corn or lentils. It is known differently in different parts of the country, namely, *chappati, parathas, naan, poori,* etc.

A majority of the Indian bread is made of wheat and can be broadly divided into three kinds: bread that is roasted on a griddle, bread that is fried, and bread that is baked. The most popular form of Indian bread is the roasted form, known as *chappati*. This kind of bread is unleavened and is made of only flour and water. At times the bread is kneaded with milk and water and is very thin. This is known as *khakra* in western India. Another variant of the roasted bread is the *roomali* which is made by stretching the dough with hand and tossing it several times in the air before roasting it.

Fried breads are also widely popular in India. These refer to the breads which are shallow-fried in fat after being rolled out into a triangular or a square-shaped size. At times there are seasonal vegetables, potatoes or fenugreek seeds that are added to the dough. These breads are generally termed *parathas*. Another type of fried bread is the *poori*. These are round, puffy and deep-fried in oil. At times poppy seeds or lentils are added to the dough to bring a different flavour to the *pooris*. These are generally served during festive occasions. Some types of Indian bread are baked in modern electric ovens or the Indian-styled ovens called tandoor. One of the popular types of baked bread is the *naan*. The dough for the naan is leavened before being baked in the tandoor. Sometimes nigella seeds or saffron water is added to give it a distinct flavour. At times garlic paste, dates, cottage cheese or almonds are also added to the dough to give it a different taste. Naan was, in Mughal times, a popular breakfast food, accompanied by *keema* or

kebab, of the humbler Muslims. It is today associated with Punjabis and is a common restaurant item rather than a homemade one, all over India.

Indian breads are always served with accompaniment like vegetables, sweet dishes, curries, pickles, and *raitas*. Bread is the staple food of a majority of the Indians. Most of the Indian households consume bread for all the three meals of the day. Indian breads comprise complex carbohydrates as well as a good amount of dietary fibre and make for a nutritious and wholesome meal.

HOW TO MAKE ROTI OR CHAPPATI

Cooking and rolling a roti is an art. To make a roti you need a griddle (*tawa*). Sprinkle a little dry flour on to a rolling board. Place the ball of dough on this and flatten. Sprinkle a little flour on top. Roll out gently to a thin pancake about 6" in diameter. Sprinkle over a tiny amount of flour, if necessary, to facilitate rolling, but not too much or the roti will turn out dry.

Put the roti on to a hot griddle and cook over high heat. When brown spots appear, turn it over and let it cook completely, particularly at the sides, pressing down. Turn it over once more so that the first side which had been slightly cooked gets completely done. Remove and wrap in foil or keep in an insulated bowl to keep them fresh before serving. (If you want to make them several hours before the meal, brush them on both sides with a little oil, fold into half and wrap into foil. Then warm in an oven just before serving.)

HANDY HINTS

- Prolonged cooking of breads for crisper, browner effect may toughen the bread and result in very dark brown specks.
- If the *paratha* cannot be served immediately, it must be kept wrapped in foil. After removing from the griddle, place the bread on a plate for about 2-3 minutes before

putting in foil. Don't pile up one above the other while hot as the heat will cause steam and affect the taste / texture of the bread.

- To reheat bread, heat the griddle on medium heat for 3 minutes. Heat one bread at a time on the griddle for a few seconds on each side. They may also be reheated in microwave oven.
- While frying the *pooris* heat sufficient oil over very high heat in a deep-frying pan, to cover the top surface of the *poori*, otherwise they will not puff up. Deep-fry the *poori* individually, turning it over in the oil. Do not add ghee or oil while making the dough of *poori*, otherwise the *pooris* will absorb too much oil during frying.

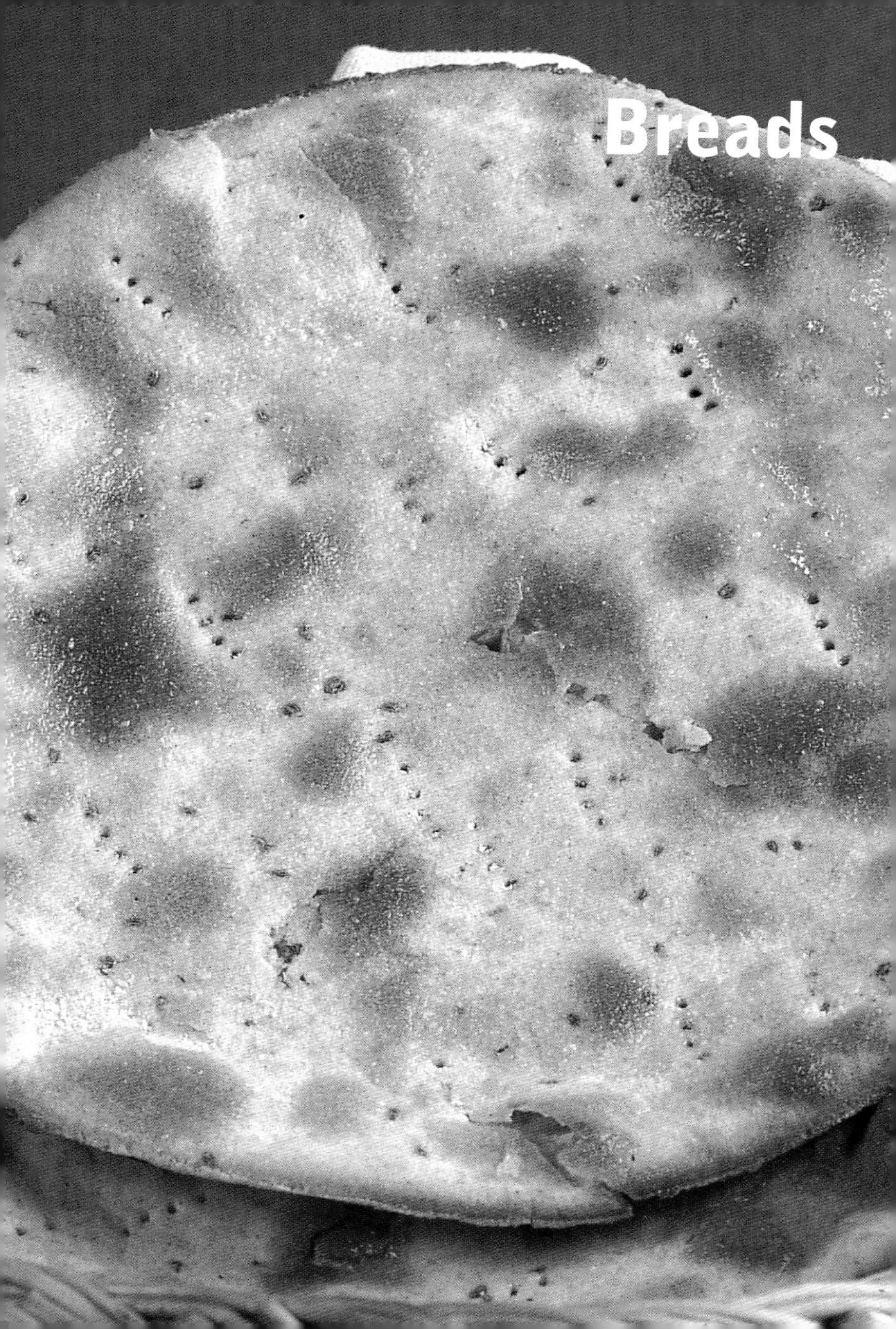

Breads

Unleavened Wholewheat Bread
Chapatti

Serves: 4-6

INGREDIENTS:

Wholewheat flour (*atta*), sieved **2 cups / 300 gm / 11 oz**
Salt (*optional*) ½ tsp / 1½ gm
Water ½ cup / **125 ml / 4 fl oz**
Ghee **1 tbsp / 15 gm**

METHOD:

Mix the wholewheat flour and salt in a bowl. Add water, knead into a smooth and elastic dough. Cover with a moist cloth and keep aside for 20 minutes at room temperature.

Place the dough on a floured board. Divide it into 8 portions, roll out each into a thin disc, the size of a snack plate.

Heat a griddle (*tawa*); place one disc on the griddle. Cook until tiny spots appear on one side, flip over and cook the other side for a few seconds. Flip over again and cook till it is pale golden on both sides.

Brush lightly with ghee and serve hot with any curry dish.

Maize Flour Bread
Makke Ki Roti

Serves: 4-6

INGREDIENTS:

Maize flour (*makke ka atta*) 2½ cups / 350 gm / 12 oz
Salt to taste
Ghee 1 tbsp / 15 gm
Fenugreek (*methi*) leaves, finely chopped 1 cup / 60 gm / 2 oz
Red chilli powder 1 tsp / 3 gm
Ghee for frying 2 tbsp / 30 gm / 1 oz
Butter 1 tbsp / 15 gm

METHOD:

Sift the maize flour and salt. Add ghee, fenugreek leaves, and red chilli powder; mix well. Make a stiff dough with hot water.

Divide the dough into 8-10 portions. Shape each out into a thick disc between your palms.

Heat the griddle (*tawa*) till hot; lay the disc flat on it and cook both sides over low heat.

When nearly done, pour a little ghee and fry both sides till golden brown. Remove from the griddle and pinch the disc in four or five places on one side. Add butter on the pinched places and serve hot. Repeat with the other discs.

Serve with mustard greens (*sarson ka saag*).

Fenugreek-Flavoured Unleavened Bread
Methi Ki Roti

Serves: 2-3

INGREDIENTS:

Wholewheat flour (*atta*) **2** cups / **300** gm / **11** oz
Fenugreek (*methi*) leaves, chopped **1** cup / **60** gm / **2** oz
Green coriander (*hara dhaniya*), chopped **1** cup / **60** gm / **2** oz
Green chillies, chopped **2**
Salt to taste
Vegetable oil for shallow-frying

METHOD:

Mix the wholewheat flour, fenugreek leaves, green coriander, green chillies, and salt together. Add 1 tbsp oil; knead with enough water to make a smooth dough. Cover and keep aside for 30 minutes.

Knead again and divide the dough into lemon-sized balls. Roll each out to a 2" disc, smear some oil on the top surface and fold into a half moon. Fold the half moon again into a triangle. Now roll the triangle out.

Heat a griddle (*tawa*); lay a triangle flat on it and cook on both sides till tiny brown spots appear. Drizzle a little oil and fry till golden brown on both sides. Remove and repeat till all the triangles are fried.

Serve hot with yoghurt and pickle of your choice.

Bread Enriched with Lentils
Missi Roti

Serves: 10

INGREDIENTS:

Bengal gram (*chana dal*), cooked, mashed into paste
½ cup / 100 gm / 3½ oz
Green gram (*moong dal*), husked, cooked, mashed into paste ½ cup / 100 gm / 3½ oz
Wholewheat flour (*atta*)
3 tbsp / 30 gm / 1 oz
Refined flour (*maida*) 2 tbsp / 20 gm
Onion, finely chopped 5 tbsp / 60 gm / 2 oz
Green chillies, finely chopped 3
Ginger (*adrak*), finely chopped 1 tbsp / 24 gm
Green coriander (*hara dhaniya*), fresh, chopped 3 tsp
Turmeric (*haldi*) powder ½ tsp / 1½ gm
Kashmiri red chilli powder 1 tsp / 3 gm
Salt to taste
Ghee 3 tbsp / 45 gm / 1½ oz

METHOD:

Mix the wheat flour and refined flour in a bowl. Add the dal pastes and the remaining ingredients expect ghee. Mix thoroughly, adding enough water, and knead into a soft pliable dough. Cover the dough with a light cloth and keep aside for about 10 minutes.

Divide the dough into 10 equal portions, shape into balls, dust with wholewheat flour, cover with a moist cloth and keep aside for another 5 minutes.

Flatten each ball between palms to a round disc, place on a cushioned pad (*gaddi*), stick inside a moderately hot tandoor and bake for about 4 minutes. Alternatively, you can place it in the pre-heated oven, on a greased baking tray and bake for about 6 minutes. Repeat till all are done.

Serve hot.

Shallow-Fried Cottage Cheese Bread
Tai Roti

Makes: 20

INGREDIENTS:

Refined flour (*maida*) 5 cups / 600 gm / 22 oz
Cottage cheese (*paneer*), grated 200 gm / 7 oz
Cabbage (*bandh gobhi*), grated 200 gm / 7 oz
Capsicum (*Shimla mirch*), big, grated 1
Salt to taste
Milk 1 cup / 250 ml / 8 fl oz
Ghee for shallow-frying

METHOD:

Mix the flour with cottage cheese, cabbage, capsicum, and salt.

Add milk, gradually, and knead into a stiff dough.

Divide the dough equally into 20 portions and roll each out to make a small disc of 4″ diameter.

Heat a griddle (*tawa*); lay a disc flat on it and roast both sides, till half done. The half done discs can be kept for 5-6 hours.

Before serving, shallow-fry the discs on a griddle till golden and crisp. The discs can be roasted on a coal fire or in a tandoor to avoid the use of ghee.

Variation: *Instead of cottage cheese, cabbage and capsicum the following combinations can be used in the above method:*
* Coarsely crushed potatoes, green peas, and cauliflower;
* Finely chopped fenugreek leaves;
* Chopped spinach and finely diced onions;
* Coarsely crushed carrots, beans and green peas.

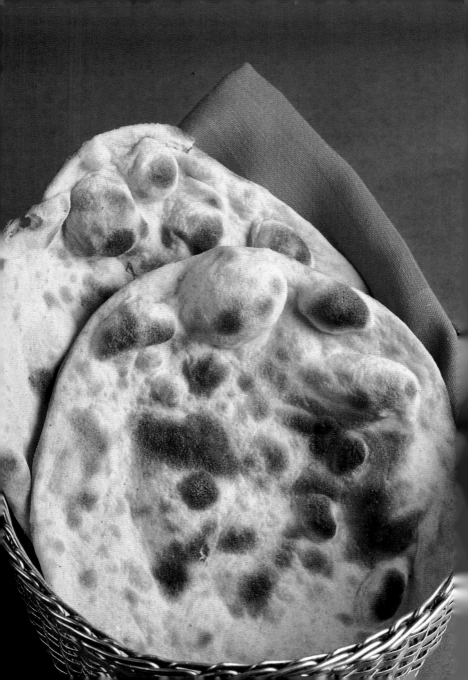

Leavened Wholewheat Bread
Khameeri Roti

Makes: 8

Wholewheat flour (*atta*) **2 cups / 300** gm / **11** oz
Salt to taste
Yeast, fresh **1½ tsp**
Ghee for greasing the baking tray
Refined flour (*maida*) to dust

METHOD:

Dissolve the yeast in ½ cup warm water.

Sift the wholewheat flour with salt onto a platter.

Make a well in the flour and pour 1 cup water. Mix flour and water gradually, then knead into a tough dough. Cover with a damp cloth and keep aside for 15 minutes.

Slowly sprinkle the dissolved yeast over the dough and keep kneading till the dough is smooth and pliable and not sticky. Cover with a damp cloth and keep aside for 30 minutes.

Divide the dough into 8 equal balls and dust with dry flour.

Press and flatten each ball into round discs, 8″ wide. Wearing an oven glove stick the disc to the side of a hot tandoor and bake for 2 minutes. Remove with a pair of tongs. Alternatively, place on a greased baking tray and bake for 4-5 minutes in a preheated oven at 180°C / 350°F. Serve hot.

INGREDIENTS:

Wholewheat flour (*atta*) **5 cups / 750 gm / 26 oz**
Salt to taste
Sugar **2 tsp / 6 gm**
Carom (*ajwain*) seeds **1 tbsp / 7½ gm**
Water **1 cup / 250 ml / 8 fl oz**

METHOD:

Sift the flour; add salt, sugar, and carom seeds. Knead into a hard dough with water. Cover with a moist cloth and keep aside for 15 minutes.

Divide the dough into 10 balls. Dust and roll each into 10 cm roti. Prick with a fork evenly.

Bake the roti in an oven at 180°C / 350°F for 8-10 minutes or till light brown in colour.

Unleavened Semolina Bread
Rawa Roti
Makes: 4-5

INGREDIENTS:

Semolina (*rawa*), fine 2 cups / 400 gm / 14 oz
Vegetable oil for frying
Mustard seeds (*rai*) ¼ tsp
Bengal gram (*chana dal*) 1 tsp
Water 2 cups / 500 ml / 16 fl oz
Ground to a paste:
Green chillies 8
Salt 1½ tsp / 4½ gm
Asafoetida (*hing*) a pinch
Onions, small, chopped ½ cup / 60 gm / 2 oz
Yoghurt (*dahi*), sour 2 tbsp / 30 gm / 1 oz
Green coriander (*hara dhaniya*), finely chopped 1½ tbsp / 6 gm
Curry leaves (*kadhi patta*) 4-5

METHOD:

Heat the oil in a frying pan (deep curved); add mustard seeds and Bengal gram. When the seeds start crackling, add water and bring to the boil. Reduce heat, add semolina and mix by stirring constantly.

Remove the pan from the heat and allow the mixture to cool. Add green chilli paste, onions, yoghurt, green coriander, and curry leaves. Knead to a thick dough.

Divide the dough equally into 4-5 balls. Pat the balls on a wet cloth or polythene sheet to make thick rotis.

Heat a griddle (*tawa*); lay a roti flat on it and fry with enough oil on both sides. Remove and repeat till all the rotis are fried.

Note: *Use fresh not roasted semolina.*

Tandoori Roti

Makes: 5

INGREDIENTS:

Wholewheat flour (*atta*) 2½ cups / 375 gm / 13 oz
Salt 1 tsp / 3 gm
Vegetable oil 1 tbsp / 15 ml
Water ½ cup / 125 ml / 4 fl oz
Butter for greasing the baking tray

METHOD:

Sift the flour and salt together. Mix in the oil and water; knead to make a soft dough. Cover with a moist cloth and keep aside for 30 minutes.

Divide the dough equally into 5 balls and dust with flour.

Heat the oven to 180°C / 350°F; flatten the balls and roll each out to an 8″ disc. Place the discs on a greased tray and bake for 3 minutes till pale brown in colour.

Serve hot.

Baked Wheat Flour Bread Dipped in Ghee
Bati

Serves: 6-8

INGREDIENTS:

Wholewheat flour (*atta*) 4 cups / 600 gm / 22 oz
Ghee 3½ tbsp / 52 gm / 1¾ oz
Salt 1 tsp / 3 gm
Sugar ½ tsp / 1½ gm
Soda bicarbonate ½ tsp / 1½ gm
Ghee to dip the *bati* in before serving

METHOD:

Sift the wholewheat flour, rub in 3 tbsp ghee. Add salt, sugar, and soda bicarbonate.

Knead with approximately ¾ cup water into a hard dough. Cover the dough with a moist cloth and keep aside for 1 hour.

Divide the dough equally into lemon-sized portions. Shape each into smooth rounds with your palms and steam for 20 minutes in an electrical steamer or in a pressure cooker (without the whistle).

Now roast them on a coal fire or in a tandoor till they are well done. Wipe with a clean cloth, dip in hot ghee and serve immediately with five-in-one dal (*panchmela dal*).

Variations: *To make stuffed* bati, *make a filling of gram flour, carom seeds, red chilli powder, and salt with a little water. Make a hollow in the centre of each round and stuff in this filling. Smoothen each round before steaming.*

Baked Wheat Flour Bread Stuffed with Green Peas
Matar Bati

Serves: 4-6

INGREDIENTS:

Bati dough (see p. 24) **1 quantity**
Green peas (*hara matar*) **150 gm / 5 oz**
Vegetable oil **4 tbsp / 60 ml / 2 fl oz**
Cumin (*jeera*) seeds **½ tsp / 1 gm**
Onion, medium-sized, chopped **1**
Coriander (*dhaniya*) powder **1 tsp / 3 gm**
Red chilli powder **½ tsp / 1½ gm**
Green chillies, chopped **1 tsp**
Tomato, medium-sized, chopped **1**
Green coriander (*hara dhaniya*), chopped **2 tbsp / 8 gm**

METHOD:

Heat the oil in a wok (*kadhai*); add cumin seeds; when they crackle, add the onion and sauté till it is well browned.

Add coriander powder, red chilli powder, green chillies, and tomato. Cook till the tomato becomes soft.

Add green peas. Lower heat and cook till they become tender and the excess liquid dries. Garnish with green coriander.

When the mixture cools, fill small portions of it in the *bati* and bake in an oven, as mentioned.

Variation: *For non-vegetarian bati, use lamb mince instead of green peas.*

Unleavened Wholewheat Fried, Puffed Bread

Poori

Makes: 25

Wholewheat flour (*atta*) **1 cup / 150 gm / 5 oz**
Salt to taste
Vegetable oil **2 tsp / 10 ml**
Water ½ cup / **125 ml / 4 fl oz**
Vegetable oil for deep-frying

Sift the wholewheat flour and salt together. Add oil and mix well.

Make a well in the flour mixture, add cold water and knead into a hard dough.

Divide the dough into 25 equal-sized balls and place them on a lightly floured surface. Cover with a kitchen cloth for 5-10 minutes.

Flatten each ball between the palms to make a disc, 4.5 cm in diameter. Roll out each of them to form a 10 cm disc.

Heat the oil in a wok (*kadhai*); deep-fry the discs until they puff up. Remove and drain on paper towels. Serve hot.

Deep-Fried Flour Bread
Luchi
Serves: 4-6

INGREDIENTS:

Refined flour (*maida*) 5 cups / 600 gm / 22 oz
Ghee ¼ cup / 50 gm / 1¾ oz
Salt ½ tsp / 1½ gm
Water ½ cup / 125 ml / 4 fl oz
Ghee for frying

METHOD:

Make a stiff dough with flour, ghee, salt, and water. Keep aside to rest for 2 hours.

Separate the dough into small round lemon-sized balls.

Roll out the balls into flat discs, about 4″ in diameter.

Heat the ghee for frying; deep-fry the discs till golden brown in colour.

Serve hot as an accompaniment.

Black Gram Stuffed Fried Bread

Bharvin Poori

Makes: 20

INGREDIENTS:

Wholewheat flour (*atta*) **5 cups / 750 gm / 26 oz**
Salt to taste
Vegetable oil **2 tbsp / 30 ml / 1 fl oz**
For the stuffing:
Whole black gram (*urad dal*), soaked
    overnight, drained **1 cup / 200 gm / 7 oz**
Asafoetida (*hing*) **a pinch**
Fennel (*moti saunf*), pounded **1 tbsp / 7½ gm**
Coriander (*dhaniya*) seeds, crushed **4 tsp / 8 gm**
Red chilli powder **1 tsp / 3 gm**
Vegetable oil for frying

METHOD:

Sift the flour and salt. Mix in the oil and knead with enough water to make a smooth dough.

For the stuffing, remove the skin of the black gram by rubbing between your palms. Grind the black gram with all the spices to a coarse, sticky paste.

Divide the flour dough equally into 20 balls. Flatten each ball, grease the top surface and add 1 tbsp paste. Bring the edges together to seal the filling. Make a ball and roll each out to a 3″ disc. Repeat with the other balls.

Heat the oil in a wok (*kadhai*); deep-fry the discs, over low heat, till golden on both sides. Remove and drain. Before serving, fry the puffs again till crisp.

Serve hot with potato curry (*aloo ki khatti tarkari*).

Shallow-Fried Bread Stuffed with Green Peas
Matar Ki Poori

Makes: 15

INGREDIENTS:

Refined four (*maida*) **3 cups / 360 gm / 12 oz**
Vegetable oil **2 tbsp / 30 ml / 1 fl oz**
For the filling:
Green peas (*hara matar*), shelled, ground to a smooth paste **400 gm / 14 oz**
Ghee **2-3 tbsp / 30-45 gm / 1-1½ oz**
Asafoetida (*hing*) **a pinch**
Salt to taste
Sugar ½ **tsp / 1½ gm**
Soda bicarbonate **a pinch**

METHOD:

For the filling, heat the ghee in a pan; add all the ingredients and sauté till the mixture leaves the sides of the wok and is not sticky to touch. Remove and divide the mixture into 15 portions.

Rub 1 tbsp oil into the refined flour and knead with enough water into a soft dough. Divide the dough equally into 15 portions.

Take a portion of the dough, make a hollow in the centre and fill a portion of the green-pea mixture. Fold over the edges to seal the filling inside. Repeat till all are done. Cover the stuffed balls with a moist cloth and keep aside for 10-15 minutes.

With the help of dry flour, roll out each ball into a thin disc of 10″ diameter.
Roast the disc on a griddle (*tawa*) on both sides using 1½ tsp oil. Remove and repeat with the other discs. Cover with aluminium foil.

Stuffed Green Gram Bread
Moong Dal Poori
Makes: 12-13

INGREDIENTS:

Refined flour (*maida*) **2 cups / 240 gm / 9 oz**
Vegetable oil **3 tbsp / 45 ml / 1½ fl oz**
Asafoetida (*hing*) **a pinch**
Cumin (*jeera*) seeds ½ tsp / **1 gm**
Split green gram (*dhuli moong dal*), soaked for 2 hours, drained and
    ground to a paste **1 cup / 200 gm / 7 oz**
Red chilli powder **2 tbsp / 14 oz**
Salt to taste
Garam masala **1 tsp / 3 gm**

METHOD:

Heat 2 tbsp oil in a pan; add asafoetida and cumin seeds, sauté for a few seconds. Add the green gram paste, and the remaining ingredients; sauté till the mixture leaves the sides of the pan and is soft.

Rub 1 tbsp oil into the refined flour and knead with enough water into a soft dough. Divide the dough equally into 12-13 portions.

Take a portion, make a hollow in the centre and fill with the green gram mixture. Seal the filling inside. Repeat with the other portions. Cover the stuffed balls with a moist cloth and keep aside for 10-15 minutes. Roll out each portion into a thin disc of 10" diameter with some dry flour.

Roast the disc on a griddle (*tawa*) on both sides with 1½ tsp oil. Remove and repeat with the other discs. Cover with aluminum foil.

Spiced Puffed Bread
Masala Poori

Serves: 5-6

Refined flour (*maida*), sieved **2 cups / 240 gm / 9** oz
Salt ½ tsp / 1½ gm
Cayenne pepper or paprika **a pinch**
Turmeric (*haldi*) powder **a pinch**
Coriander (*dhaniya*) powder **2 tsp / 6 gm**
Cumin (*jeera*) powder 1½ tsp / 4½ gm
Vegetable oil ½ **tbsp / 8 ml**
Water, warm **150 ml / 5 fl** oz
Vegetable oil for frying

Mix the refined flour, salt, cayenne pepper, turmeric powder, coriander powder, and cumin powder. Add oil and mix till it is well incorporated. Add water, knead into a medium-soft dough.

Lightly grease your palms and knead until the dough is smooth and pliable. Brush with oil and keep aside for 3 hours.

Knead again briefly and divide the dough into 16 equal portions; shape each into balls. Compress each into a 2" patty. Dip one end of the patty in oil and roll out into a 5" round; place on a flat surface. Similarly, roll out the other portions.

Heat the oil in a wok (*kadhai*); fry one round at a time until it puffs up and is golden brown on both sides. Remove and serve hot.

INGREDIENTS:

Refined flour (*maida*) **4 cups / 480 gm / 17 oz**
Baking powder **1 tsp / 3 gm**
Salt **1 tsp / 3 gm**
Sugar **1 tsp / 3 gm**
Yoghurt (*dahi*) **1 cup / 250 gm / 9 oz**
Warm water **6 tbsp / 90 ml / 3 fl oz**
Ghee **1 tbsp / 15 gm**
Vegetable oil for frying

METHOD:

Sift the refined flour, baking powder, and salt together. Add sugar, yoghurt, and warm water to make a smooth dough. Grease your palms with 1 tbsp oil and continue to knead till the dough becomes pliable. Cover with a moist cloth and keep aside for 2 hours.

Divide the dough into 12 lemon-sized balls. Roll them out into discs of 4" diameter.

Heat the oil in a wok (*kadhai*); fry each disc until it puffs up. Turn and cook the other side too. Remove with a slotted spoon and drain the excess oil on absorbent kitchen towels.

Serve hot with spicy chickpeas (Punjabi *chana*).

Crispy Flour Puffs
Khasta Kachori

Makes: 16

INGREDIENTS:

Refined flour (*maida*) **2 cups / 240 gm / 7 oz**
Salt to taste
Soda bicarbonate **a pinch**
Ghee **1 tbsp / 15 gm**
For the filling:
Split black gram (*dhuli urad dal*), washed, soaked
   for 2 hours, drained **1 cup / 200 gm / 7 oz**
Cumin (*jeera*) seeds **1 tsp / 2 gm**
Asafoetida (*hing*) **a pinch**
Coriander (*dhaniya*) powder **2 tsp / 6 gm**
Red chilli powder **½ tsp / 1½ gm**
Salt **1 tsp / 3 gm**
Vegetable oil for frying

METHOD:

Sift the flour, salt, and soda bicarbonate. Rub in the ghee and knead with enough water to make a hard dough. Keep aside for 30 minutes.

For the filling, grind all the ingredients together coarsely on a stone slab or in a mixer. Sauté the filling in 1 tbsp ghee till golden. Keep aside to cool.

Divide the flour dough into 16 balls. Shape each ball into a small cup; fill 1 tbsp filling into the hollow, pinch together to seal and pat into rounds.

Heat the oil in a wok (*kadhai*); deep-fry the rounds, a few at a time, over low heat till they puff up and become crisp and golden. Remove and drain the excess oil on absorbent kitchen paper towels. Serve hot.

40

Fried Black Gram Bread
Urad Kachori

Makes: 30

INGREDIENTS:

Black gram (*urad dal*), soaked for 1½ hours ½ cup / 100 gm / 3½ oz
Refined flour (*maida*) 2 cups / 240 gm / 8 oz
Semolina (*suji*) 1 cup / 200 gm / 7 oz
Asafoetida (*hing*) a pinch
Onion seeds (*kalonji*) ½ pinch
Salt to taste
Vegetable oil 1½ tbsp / 22 ml

METHOD:

Drain the black gram and grind to a smooth paste.

Mix black gram paste with the remaining ingredients. Add a little water and knead to make a soft dough. Keep aside for 1 hour.

Before frying, knead the dough again with well-greased palms and on a well-greased table top. Divide the dough into lemon-sized balls. Roll each ball out carefully into a 5″ diameter disc.

Heat the oil in a wok (*kadhai*); fry the discs, one by one, turning them over frequently, on high heat till golden. They will be slightly white on the edges. Remove with a slotted spoon and drain the excess oil on paper towels.

Serve hot with spiced potatoes (*aloo dum*).

Green Pea Puffs
Motor Chuti Kachori

Serves: 2-4

INGREDIENTS:

Green peas (*hara matar*), shelled 500 gm / 1.1 lb
Cumin (*jeera*) seeds 2 tbsp / 18 gm
Dry red chillies (*sookhi lal mirch*) 4 tsp / 20 gm
Green cardamom (*choti elaichi*) 2 tsp / 10 gm
Ghee 2 tbsp / 30 gm / 1 oz
Salt to taste
Red chilli powder 2 tbsp / 14 gm
Refined flour (*maida*) 1½ cups / 180 gm / 6 oz
Water 4 tbsp / 60 ml / 2 fl oz
Ghee 2 tbsp / 30 gm / 1 oz
Vegetable oil / Ghee for frying

METHOD:

Grind the green peas into a paste.

Broil the cumin seeds, dry red chillies, and green cardamom. Then powder them. Keep aside.

Heat the ghee in a pan; cook the green pea paste with salt, red chilli powder, and the broiled powder. Keep the stuffing aside.

Make a stiff dough by using flour, water, and ghee. Allow the dough to rest for 2 hours in the fridge.

Divide the dough into equal-sized balls. Take each ball, make a well in the middle, add the stuffing and cover it. Shape like small patties and deep-fry till golden. Serve hot.

Refined flour (*maida*)
   4 cups / 480 gm / 17 oz
Salt 1 tsp / 3 gm
Ghee 4 tbsp / 60 gm / 2 oz
Yoghurt (*dahi*) 2 tbsp / 30 gm / 1 oz
Water, chilled ½ cup / 125 ml / 4 fl oz
Green chillies, deseeded, finely
   chopped 2-3
Ginger (*adrak*), finely
   chopped 1½ tsp / 9 gm
Potatoes, boiled,
   mashed 300 gm / 11 oz

Coriander (*dhaniya*) powder 1 tsp / 3 gm
Cumin (*jeera*) powder 1 tsp / 3 gm
Fennel (*moti saunf*), ground ½ tsp
Garam masala 1 tsp / 3 gm
Turmeric (*haldi*) powder a pinch
Lemon (*nimbu*) juice 1 tbsp / 15 ml
Salt 1 tsp / 3 gm
Green coriander (*hara dhaniya*),
   finely chopped 2 tbsp / 8 gm
Vegetable oil for frying

METHOD:

Mix the flour and salt in a mixing bowl. Add ghee, rub until fully incorporated and the mixture resembles coarse breadcrumbs. Add yoghurt and 6 tbsp chilled water; knead to make a smooth and pliable dough. Cover with plastic wrap and keep aside for half an hour.

Combine the remaining ingredients except oil in a mixing bowl and knead with hands until well blended. Divide into 18 portions; keep aside.

Divide the dough equally into 18 portions. Shape each portion into a patty. Cover with a damp towel or plastic wrap and set aside.

Flatten each patty into a 2½" or 6.5 cm round. Place one portion of filling in the centre of the dough, then bring the sides of the dough over the filling to enclose completely. Pinch the seams together until thoroughly sealed. Cover with a plastic wrap or a moist towel. Keep aside. Shape and stuff the remaining patties.

Heat the oil in a wok (kadhai) till it starts smoking. Slip in a few patties (seam-side down) at a time. Fry until pale golden in colour and until they sound hollow when tapped. The crust should be delicately blistered and crisp. Drain excess oil and serve hot, accompanied by tomato ketchup.

Unleavened Bread
Fried on a Griddle
Paratha

Makes: 5

INGREDIENTS:

Wholewheat flour (*atta*) 5 cups / 750 gm / 26 oz
Salt to taste
Ghee 1 cup / 200 gm / 7 oz
Water 1 cup / 250 ml / 8 fl oz

METHOD:

Sift the wholewheat flour and salt in a bowl, incorporate 2 tbsp ghee, add the water gradually, and knead to a smooth dough.

Divide the dough into 5 equal portions and shape each into balls. Dust each with flour, cover with a damp cloth and keep aside for 10 minutes.

Flatten each ball and roll out. Brush with ghee and fold over. Brush the folded surface with ghee and fold over again to form a triangle. Roll out the triangle with a rolling pin.

Heat a griddle (*tawa*) and brush the surface with ghee. Place the *paratha* on the griddle and fry for a few minutes. Coat with a little ghee, turn over and fry the other side as well. Both sides of the *paratha* should be crisp and delicately browned.

Remove and serve immediately.

INGREDIENTS:

Wholewheat flour (*atta*) ½ cup / 75 gm / 2½ oz
Ghee 1 tbsp / 15 gm

For the filling:
Potatoes, boiled, mashed 1 cup
Garam masala ½ tsp / 1½ gm
Red chilli powder ¾ tsp / 2 gm
Coriander (*dhaniya*) seeds, roasted, powdered 1 tsp / 2 gm
Green coriander (*hara dhaniya*), chopped 1 tbsp / 4 gm
Onion, chopped 1 tbsp / 12 gm
Salt to taste
Ghee for shallow-frying

METHOD:

Sift the wholewheat flour. Rub in the ghee with the fingertips. Knead with enough cold water to make a soft dough.

For the filling, mix all the ingredients together. Divide the filling into 10 equal portions.

Divide the dough equally into 10 portions. Flatten each out into a small disc. Place 1 portion of the filling in the centre, press the edges to seal and reshape into a ball. Roll each ball out into an 8″ disc, dusting with dry flour to prevent sticking.

Heat a griddle (*tawa*); cook the disc, drizzling 1 tsp ghee, till tiny brown spots appear on both sides. Similarly repeat with the other discs.

Serve hot with yoghurt, chutney and pickle.

Shallow Fried Layered Unleavened Bread
Lachha Paratha

Serves: 4

INGREDIENTS:

Refined flour (*maida*) 4 cups / 480 gm / 17 oz
Salt to taste
Milk 1 cup / 250 ml / 9 fl oz
Fennel (*moti saunf*), pounded 2 tsp / 5 gm
Ghee ¾ cup / 150 gm / 5 oz
Ghee for shallow-frying
Water ½ cup / 125 ml / 4 fl oz

METHOD:

Sift flour and salt together. Make a well in the mixture and pour in the milk and water. Mix gradually and knead into a dough. Cover with a moist cloth and keep aside for 10 minutes.

Melt ½ cup ghee, add to the dough, kneading constantly to make it soft and smooth.

Add fennel and knead again for 5 minutes.

Divide into 12 equal balls, dust lightly and roll into 6″ discs. Apply 1 tsp ghee evenly over one side.

Make a radial cut and fold the disc into a narrow conical shape. Place flat side of the cone on the palm and twist palms together in a round movement to compress the dough into a thick flat round (*pedha*). Dust with flour, roll it out into an 8″ disc. Refrigerate for an hour on butter paper.

Heat the griddle and shallow-fry the *paratha* on both sides on low heat till golden.

Serve hot with *raita* (see p. 92).

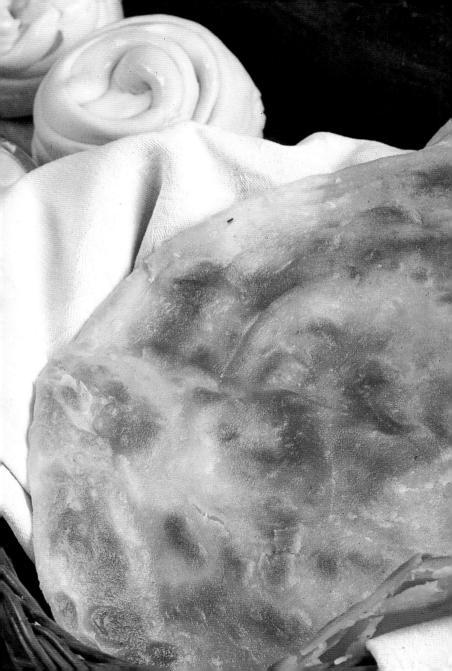

INGREDIENTS:

Wholewheat flour (*atta*) 5 cups / 750 gm / 26 oz
Salt 1 tsp / 3 gm
Ghee ¾ cup / 150 gm / 5 oz
Water 1 cup / 250 ml / 8 fl oz
Mint (*pudina*) leaves, dried 1 tbsp / 4 gm

METHOD:

Mix the wholewheat flour with salt and half of the ghee. Add water and knead to a smooth dough. Cover and keep aside for 30 minutes.

Shape the dough into a ball, roll out into a big, round disc. Smear the remaining ghee and sprinkle dried mint leaves.

Pleat the dough into 1 collected strip. Divide equally into lemon-sized portions and roll each out into 6"-diameter pancake.

Heat a griddle (*tawa*) / tandoor and cook till brown spots appear on both sides.

Remove and serve hot.

Shallow-Fried Layered Bread
Malabar Parotta

INGREDIENTS:

Refined flour (*maida*) 2 cups / 240 gm / 8 oz
Baking powder 1 tsp / 3 gm
Ghee 6 tbsp / 90 gm / 3 oz
Salt to taste
Water as required

METHOD:

Sift the refined flour and baking powder.

Add 1½ tbsp ghee and rub well till well incorporated. Add salt and enough water (approximately ¾ cup) and knead well to form a soft dough.

Divide the dough equally into 8 balls. Roll each out into a thin disc and smear ghee over the surface. Then roll the disc from one end to the other and then coil it around. Repeat with the other balls. Keep aside for 15 minutes.

Roll the coils again into thin discs.

Heat the griddle (*tawa*) over low heat; place a disc flat over it and cook for a few minutes. Turn the disc over and smear some ghee over and around it. Turn again and do the same on the other side and fry till both sides are golden brown. Remove and repeat till all are done.

Serve hot.

INGREDIENTS:

Wholewheat flour (*atta*) 2 cups / 300 gm / 11 oz
Cumin (*jeera*) seeds, roasted, coarsely powdered ¾ tsp / 1½ gm
Salt 1 tsp / 3 gm
Red chilli powder 1 tsp / 3 gm
Mango powder (*amchur*) ½ tsp / 1½ gm
Garam masala ½ tsp / 1½ gm
Yoghurt (*dahi*), fresh, thick ½ cup / 125 gm / 4 oz
Milk ½ cup / 125 ml / 4 fl oz
Vegetable oil for the dough 5 tsp / 25 ml
Vegetable oil for frying

METHOD:

Mix all the dry ingredients together in a mixing bowl.

Pour yoghurt, milk, and oil; knead to a smooth dough. Keep the dough covered for 3-4 hours.

Divide the dough equally into 4-5 portions. Roll each portion out into a thick disc.

Heat a griddle (*tawa*); lay the disc flat on it and fry on both sides till light brown. Remove and repeat till all are fried.

Shallow-Fried Bread Encased with Egg

Anda Paratha

Serves: 4

INGREDIENTS:

Wholewheat flour (*atta*)
  2 cups / 300 gm / 11 oz
Ghee **1 tbsp / 15 gm**
Eggs, beaten **4**
Onions, small, chopped **2**

Green coriander (*hara dhaniya*),
  chopped **a sprig**
Salt to taste
Green chillies **2-3**
Vegetable oil for shallow-frying

METHOD:

Beat the eggs with onions, green coriander, salt, and green chillies. Keep aside.

Mix the wholewheat flour with 1 tbsp ghee and a little salt and knead with a little water to obtain a medium-soft dough.

Divide the dough equally into even-sized balls. Dust these balls with a little flour and roll out into discs of about 7" diameter. Brush lightly with ghee. Sprinkle over a little dry flour. Now fold ⅓ of the disc from one side and fold the other side over this. Sprinkle some more dry flour. Once again fold a portion from one side overlapping it with the other side to obtain a layered square. Dust it slightly again with flour and roll out into a 6" square bread.

Heat a little oil on a griddle (*tawa*); shallow-fry the *paratha* on both sides for about a minute. When the *paratha* is evenly fried and is rich golden in colour remove it to a plate and make a slit on one side with a sharp knife to create an envelope.

Spread some of the egg mixture inside and seal the opening by pressing on it. Place the *paratha* once again on the griddle and shallow-fry applying very little oil.

Repeat till all are fried.

Spicy Peas and Cottage Cheese Stuffed Bread
Matar Paneer Paratha

Makes: 8-10

INGREDIENTS:

Green peas (*hara matar*), shelled,
  boiled, mashed **1 cup / 150 gm / 5 oz**
Cottage cheese (*paneer*), crumbled **1 cup**
Ginger-chilli (*adrak-mirch*)
  paste **1 tbsp / 18 gm**
Green coriander (*hara dhaniya*),
  chopped **1 tbsp / 4 gm**
Yoghurt (*dahi*), sour,
  hung **½ cup / 125 gm / 4 oz**
Asafoetida (*hing*) **a large pinch**

Sugar **1 tsp / 3 gm**
Kashmiri red chilli
  powder **½ tsp / 1½ gm**
Garam masala **1 tsp / 3 gm**
Salt to taste
Cream of wheat,
  roasted **500 gm / 1.1 lb**
Wheat flour to dust and roll
Ghee for frying **1 cup / 200 gm / 7 oz**

METHOD:

Mix the green peas with cottage cheese, ginger-chilli paste, green coriander, yoghurt, asafoetida, sugar, red chilli powder, garam masala, and salt. Keep aside.

Mix the flour with water and knead to obtain a semi-stiff dough. Divide the dough into walnut-sized balls and lightly roll these on the floured surface into discs of about 6″ diameter.

Place equal portions of the green pea mixture in the centre of the discs and shape into small balls; roll again into discs.

Heat a little ghee on a griddle (*tawa*) and shallow-fry the *paratha* on both sides till golden brown. Serve hot.

Unleavened Bread Cooked on Inverted Griddle

Ultey Tawe Ka Paratha

Makes: 6-8

INGREDIENTS:

Refined flour (*maida*) 4¼ cups / 500 gm / 1.1 lb
Salt to taste
Cashew nut (*kaju*) paste 3¼ tbsp / 50 gm / 1¾ oz
Sugar 1½ tbsp / 18 gm
Milk 1 cup / 250 ml / 8 fl oz
Baking powder 1 tsp / 3 gm
Ghee ⅔ cup / 125 gm / 4 oz

METHOD:

Blend cashew nut paste, sugar, milk, and baking powder together. Mix with flour and salt mixture and knead to obtain a spongy dough.

Divide the dough into 6-8 portions and place them on a floured surface. Roll each portion out into a round 8" disc. Apply 1 tsp melted ghee evenly over it and dust with flour. Make a radial cut with a knife and starting with one end of the cut, roll the disc firmly into a conical shape. Hold each one between thumb and forefinger, ½" above the base, and make spiral movements to compress the rest of the cone to make a ball. Dust with flour and roll again.

Place the disc on a pre-heated inverted griddle (*tawa*), apply ghee and press the disc with a dry cloth from all sides until light brown. Apply ghee and remove. Repeat with the other discs. Serve hot.

Deep-Fried Leavened Flour Bread
Badshahi Naan

Makes: 16

INGREDIENTS:

Refined flour (*maida*) 1 kg / 2.2 lb
Yeast, granulated 2 tsp / 6 gm
Sugar 2 tsp / 6 gm
Water, lukewarm 1 cup / 250 ml / 8 fl oz
Salt to taste
Butter 4 tsp / 20 gm
Milk, warm 1 cup / 250 ml / 8 fl oz
Eggs, beaten 2
Onion seeds (*kalonji*) 1 tsp / 3 gm
Ghee for deep-frying

METHOD:

Mix the yeast, sugar, and water together. Keep aside for 10 minutes.

Sift the flour and salt. Rub in the butter till the mixture becomes crumbly.

Add the yeast mixture, milk, and eggs; knead into a smooth, elastic dough. Cover with a damp cloth and keep in a warm place to rise. It should rise to almost double its volume.

Knead again and divide the dough into 16 balls. Roll each out into a ¾"-thick disc. Lay the discs on a greased tray; sprinkle onion seeds. Let the discs rise again till they double in size.

Deep-fry the discs in a wok till golden brown. Remove and drain the excess oil. Serve hot.

A light, Leavened Bread
Naan

Serves: 4

INGREDIENTS:

Refined flour (*maida*) 2 cups / 240 gm / 8 oz
Salt to taste
Baking soda ¼ tsp
Baking powder 1 tsp / 3 gm
Whisk together:
Milk 3 tbsp / 45 ml / 1½ fl oz
Sugar 2 tsp / 6 gm
Yoghurt (*dahi*) 5 tsp / 25 gm
Vegetable oil 2 tbsp / 30 ml / 1 fl oz
Onion seeds (*kalonji*) 1 tsp / 2½ gm
Melon (*magaz*) seeds 1 tsp / 3 gm
Ghee for greasing the baking tray
White butter 2 tbsp / 30 gm / 2 oz

METHOD:

Sieve the first 4 ingredients onto a kneading platter. Make a well in the centre; mix in 1 cup water and milk mixture and knead to make a dough. Cover with a moist cloth and keep aside for 10 minutes.

Add oil and knead again. Cover the dough and keep aside for 2 hours till it rises. Divide the dough into 6 balls. Flatten balls and sprinkle onion and melon seeds. Cover and keep aside for 5 minutes.

Roll and flatten each ball between your palms. Stretch the dough to one side to give an elongated shape (*naan*). Using oven gloves, stick the *naan* inside a hot tandoor for 3 minutes or place the *naan* on a greased tray and bake in an oven for 10 minutes at 180°C / 350°F. Apply butter (optional) and serve.

Rich, Leavened Rice Flour Bread
Taftan

Makes: 4

INGREDIENTS:

Rice flour 2 cups / 240 gm / 8 oz
Salt to taste
Water ½ cup / 125 ml / 4 oz
Sugar ½ tsp / 1½ gm
Milk 1 cup / 250 ml / 8 fl oz
Ghee ¾ cup / 150 gm / 5 oz
Yeast ½ tsp
Melon (*magaz*) seeds 2 tsp / 4 gm
Green coriander (*hara dhaniya*), chopped 1 tbsp / 4 gm
Butter / Ghee for brushing

METHOD:

Sift flour and salt together.

Make a well in the flour and add water, sugar, milk, ghee, yeast, and melon seeds. Mix gradually and knead into a soft dough.

Divide into 4 equal balls and keep aside for half an hour.

Dust lightly and roll into 3½" discs, ¼" thick. Sprinkle with green coriander.

Put into a tandoor and bake till brown.

Brush with ghee. Serve hot.

Cardamom-Flavoured
Leavened Bread
Bakar Khani

Serves: 4

Refined flour (*maida*) 3 cups / 360 gm / 12 oz
Semolina (*suji*) 1 cup / 200 gm / 7 oz
Milk 4 tbsp / 60 ml / 2 fl oz
Ghee 2 tbsp / 30 gm / 1 oz
Green cardamom (*choti elaichi*) powder 3 tsp / 9 gm
Ginger powder (*sonth*) 2 tsp / 6 gm
Sugar 7 tsp / 20 gm
Salt 2 tsp / 6 gm
Water as required
Butter ½ cup / 100 gm / 3½ oz

METHOD:

Mix the refined flour, semolina, milk, ghee, green cardamom powder, dry ginger powder, sugar, and salt thoroughly.

Gradually, add water and knead into a smooth dough. Divide the dough equally into 8 portions and shape each into balls. Roll out each ball into a 6″ diameter.

Cook in a tandoor or a griddle (*tawa*) until brown on all sides.

Remove from the tandoor or griddle, smear butter and serve hot.

Plain Baked Bread
Sada Kulcha
Makes: 10

INGREDIENTS:

Milk **1 cup / 250 ml / 8 fl oz**
Sugar **1 tsp / 3 gm**
Yeast **3 tsp**
Refined flour (*maida*) **4 cups / 480 gm / 17 oz**
Salt **1 tsp / 3 gm**
Ghee **1 tbsp / 15 gm**
Yoghurt (*dahi*) **4 tbsp / 60 gm / 2 oz**
Water **½ cup / 125 ml / 4 fl oz**
Poppy seeds (*khus khus*) **2 tbsp / 18 gm**

METHOD:

Warm the milk in a pan; add sugar and yeast. Remove from heat and leave aside to froth for 20 minutes.

Sift the flour with salt. Pour the yeast mixture and ghee. Mix well. Slowly add the yoghurt and knead into a soft dough. Cover with a moist cloth and leave aside for 6 hours.

Knead well again, if required, and add a little warm water. Divide the dough into 10 lemon-sized portions and roll them out into thick discs of 5″ diameter. Place them on a baking tray. Cover with a damp cloth for another 30 minutes to rise.

Brush the top with a little milk or ghee and sprinkle with poppy seeds.

Bake in a preheated oven for 10 minutes. Remove and shallow fry on a griddle (*tawa*) with oil till golden.

Delicious Rich Leavened Bread
Sheermal

Makes: 12

INGREDIENTS:

Refined flour (*maida*), sieved **4 cups / 480 gm / 17 oz**
Salt to taste
Milk **1 cup / 250 ml / 8 fl oz**
Sugar **2 tsp / 6 gm**
Vetivier (*kewda*) essence **2 drops**
Ghee, melted **1 cup / 200 gm / 7 oz**
Saffron (*kesar*), dissolved in 1 tbsp milk **a pinch**
White butter for brushing

METHOD:

Heat the milk, add the sugar and stir till it dissolves completely. When cool, add the vetivier essence.

Mix the salt with the flour. Add sweetened milk and knead into a soft dough. Cover with a moist cloth and keep aside for 10 minutes.

Remove the cloth and knead the dough again, with small amounts of ghee, at a time.

Divide the dough equally into 12 balls. Cover and keep aside for 10 minutes. Roll out the balls into 8"-round discs. Prick all over with a fork. Arrange them on a greased baking tray and bake in a preheated oven at 180°C / 350°F for 4 minutes. Remove, brush with saffron and bake again for 4 minutes.

Serve immediately smeared with white butter.

INGREDIENTS:

Rice, raw **2 cups / 400 gm / 14 oz**
Rice, cooked **1 cup**
Sugar **2 tbsp / 30 gm / 1 oz**
Coconut (*nariyal*), grated **1 cup / 80 gm / 2¾ oz**
Yeast ½ **tsp**
Vegetable oil for shallow-frying

METHOD:

Grind the raw and cooked rice, sugar, coconut with enough water to make a batter of pouring consistency.

Mix in the yeast and leave the batter to ferment overnight.

Heat a heavy-bottomed vessel; rub a little oil and pour 2 tbsp batter. Twirl the vessel around till the batter coats it. Sprinkle some oil and cook covered for 2 minutes or till the base is golden and the top surface is soft and pale. Remove and repeat with the remaining batter.

Serve hot with lamb stew or egg masala.

String Hoppers
Idiappam

Serves: 4

INGREDIENTS:

Rice flour 1 cup / 120 gm / 4 oz
Water 1 cup / 250 ml / 8 fl oz
Salt to taste
Vegetable oil 1½ tbsp / 22 ml

METHOD:

Boil the water, salt, and oil in a covered vessel. Lower heat and slowly add the rice flour; mix continuously so that the mixture is lump-free.

Remove the vessel from the heat. Knead the mixture with pressure. Put some dough into a vermicelli press and press onto a muslin cloth.

Steam for 3 minutes in a steamer or till cooked.

Repeat till all the dough has been used.

Thin Chapatti Flavoured with Fenugreek
Methi Na Thepla

Serves: 4-5

INGREDIENTS:

Fenugreek (*methi*) leaves, finely chopped 1 cup / 60 gm / 2 oz
Wholewheat flour (*atta*) 2 cups / 300 gm / 11 oz
Vegetable oil 3 tbsp / 45 ml / 1½ fl oz
Cumin (*jeera*) powder ½ tsp / 1½ gm
Coriander (*dhaniya*) powder ½ tsp / 1½ gm
Turmeric (*haldi*) powder ½ tsp / 1½ gm
Red chilli powder 1 tsp / 3 gm
Salt to taste
Vegetable oil for shallow-frying

METHOD:

Mix the fenugreek leaves with the wholewheat flour. Add all the other ingredients (except oil for frying), knead with just enough water to make a medium-soft dough.

Divide the dough equally into small, round balls. Roll out each ball into a very thin disc.

Heat a griddle (*tawa*) on high heat; lower heat, lay a disc flat over it and cook on both sides till small bubbles appear on the surface.

Increase heat to medium; sprinkle ½ tbsp oil around and ¼ tbsp oil over the disc. Fry on both sides till small brown spots appear. Remove and repeat with the other discs.

Serve warm or cold at tea time.

Millet Flour Chapatti Flavoured with Fenugreek

Methi Na Dhebra

Serves: 4-5

INGREDIENTS:

Fenugreek leaves (*methi*),
   chopped 1 cup / 60 gm / 2 oz
Millet flour (*bajre ka atta*)
   1 cup / 150 gm / 5 oz
Wholewheat flour (*atta*) ¼ cup / 25 gm
Gram flour (*besan*) 1 tbsp / 10 gm
Red chilli powder ½ tsp / 1½ gm
Asafoetida (*hing*) ¼ tsp / 1½ gm
Semolina (*suji*) ¼ tsp

Yoghurt (*dahi*),
   fresh ½ cup / 125 gm / 4 oz
Garlic (*lasan*), fresh,
   chopped 1 tbsp / 12 gm
Green chillies, small, chopped 3
Vegetable oil 1 tbsp / 15 ml
Sugar 1 tsp / 3 gm
Salt to taste
Vegetable oil for shallow-frying

METHOD:

Mix all the ingredients (except oil) and knead with just enough water to make a soft dough.

Divide the dough equally into small balls. Roll each ball out into a 4″ disc.

Heat a griddle (*tawa*) on high heat. Lower heat to minimum and lay a disc flat over it; cook on both sides till small bubbles appear on the surface. Increase heat to medium; sprinkle ½ tbsp oil around the disc and ¼ tbsp oil on the surface of the disc. Fry till small brown spots appear on both sides. Remove from the griddle at once.

Repeat till all the discs are ready. Serve warm or cold at tea time.

INGREDIENTS:

Refined flour (*maida*) **2 cups / 240 gm / 8 oz**
Ghee for frying
Water to make dough

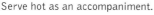

METHOD:

Knead the flour with just enough water to make a stiff dough.

Smear a little ghee on the dough and keep aside for a while.

Make small balls of the dough and roll them into thin rounds, 6" in diameter.

Heat the ghee and fry the rounds. Remove immediately; do not brown. Fold them in half and put aside, covered, so that they do not get crisp.

Serve hot as an accompaniment.

Rice Bread from Malabar
Pathri
Serves: 4-6

Rice flour **2 cups / 240 gm / 8 oz**
Cumin (*jeera*) powder ½ **tsp / 1½ gm**
Red chilli powder to taste
Salt to taste
Ghee **2 tbsp / 30 gm / 1 oz**

METHOD:

Dry roast the rice flour, cumin powder, and red chilli powder for 4-5 minutes. Add salt and a little water and knead into a soft dough.

Divide the dough into 3 cm balls, then roll each out into thin rounds.

Place the rounds flat on a frying pan. Add 1 tsp ghee and cook till the bread is slightly brown on both sides.

Smear with ghee again and serve with any curry.

Accompaniments

Mango Cooked in Jaggery
Ambakalio

Serves: 4-6

INGREDIENTS:

Mango, large, peeled, sliced **1**
Ghee / Butter **3** tbsp / **45** gm / **1½** oz
Onion, large, sliced **1**
Cinnamon (*dalchini*), 1" stick **1**
Cloves (*laung*) **4-6**
Green cardamom (*choti elaichi*) **4-6**
Jaggery (*gur*) **6¼** tsp / **125** gm / **4** oz
Green chillies, seeded, chopped **2**
Green coriander (*hara dhaniya*), chopped **1** tbsp / **4** gm
Salt ½ tsp / **1½** gm
Water ½ cup / **125** ml / **4** fl oz

METHOD:

Heat the ghee / butter in a pan; add onion, cinnamon stick, cloves, and green cardamom. Sauté till light brown.

Add jaggery, mango, green chillies, green coriander, salt, and water. Simmer for 1-2 minutes and mix gently without breaking the mango slices.

Serve as an accompaniment with bread of your choice.

INGREDIENTS:

Green mangoes, large, raw, peeled, sliced 2 kg / 4.4 lb
Sugar 2 kg / 4.4 lb
Aniseed (*saunf*) 4 tbsp / 30 gm / 1 oz
Salt 2 tbsp / 16 gm
Red chilli powder to taste
Dry red chillies (*sookhi lal mirch*) to taste
Malt vinegar (*sirka*) 1 cup / 200 ml / 7 fl oz

METHOD:

Mix the sugar and mangoes together thoroughly in a large pan.

Add the remaining ingredients (except vinegar) and cook on low heat till the sugar dissolves.

When the mangoes are soft, add malt vinegar. Cook for a few minutes till the syrup is quite thick.

Be careful not to over cook as the consistency will become thick when the mixture cools. Store in airtight jars.

Tamarind Chutney
Imli Ki Chutney

Serves: 6-8

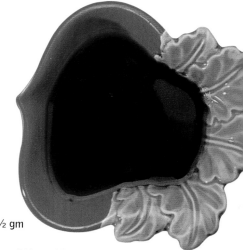

INGREDIENTS:

Tamarind (*imli*) **100** gm / **3½** oz
Jaggery (*gur*) **200** gm / **7** oz
Black salt (*kala namak*) **1½** tsp / **4½** gm
Salt **2** tsp / **6** gm
Cumin (*jeera*) seeds, roasted, powdered **1½** tsp / **3** gm
Green cardamom (*choti elaichi*), powdered **4-5**
Ginger powder (*sonth*) **½** tsp / **1½** gm

METHOD:

Soak the tamarind and jaggery together for 4-5 hours.

Mash the two thoroughly with a wooden spoon or rub between your palms. Strain through a muslin cloth.

Add the remaining ingredients and bring the mixture to the boil, stirring continuously.

Cool and preserve.

Note: *If refrigerated, this can stay for about 15-20 days.*

Garlic Relish
Lasan Chutney

Serves: 6-8

INGREDIENTS:

Garlic (*lasan*) cloves, thick **15-16**
Red chilli powder **2 tbsp / 14 gm**
White vinegar (*sirka*) **4 tbsp / 60 ml / 2 fl oz**
Salt to taste
Vegetable oil **5 tbsp / 75 ml / 2½ fl oz**

METHOD:

Mix all the ingredients together except the oil and blend to a smooth paste.

Heat the oil in a pan; sauté the garlic paste for 2-3 minutes. Remove the pan from the heat.

Cool and preserve.

Green Coriander Relish
Hare Dhaniye Ki Chutney

Serves: 6-8

INGREDIENTS:

Green coriander (*hara dhaniya*) 1½ cups / 90 gm / 3 oz
Green chillies 2
Ginger (*adrak*), 1" piece 1
Garlic (*lasan*) cloves (optional) 2
Cumin (*jeera*) seeds ½ tsp / 1 gm
Lemon (*nimbu*) juice 1

METHOD:

Blend all the ingredients except the lemon juice to a smooth paste.

Store the relish in a dry glass jar, in the refrigerator.

Just before serving, add lemon juice, mix well and serve as an accompaniment.

Note: *If garlic is used then omit cumin seeds.*

Mint Chutney with Yoghurt
Pudina Chutney
Serves: 4

INGREDIENTS:

Mint (*pudina*) leaves, chopped 1½ cups / 90 gm / 3 oz
Green coriander (*hara dhaniya*), chopped 1½ cups / 90 gm / 3 oz
Onions, chopped 2 tbsp / 24 gm
Ginger (*adrak*), chopped 1 tbsp / 24 gm
Green chillies, chopped 4-5
Yoghurt (*dahi*) ½ cup / 125 gm / 4 oz
Mango powder (*amchur*) 1 tsp / 2 gm
Sugar 1 tbsp / 12 gm
Salt to taste
Black salt (*kala namak*) 1 tsp / 4 gm

METHOD:

Blend the mint leaves, green coriander, onions, ginger, and green chillies to make a smooth paste. Keep aside.

In a mixing bowl, whisk yoghurt with mango powder, sugar, salt, and rock salt. Add the mint paste and mix well.

Serve with kebabs and Indian breads.

Lemon Pickle
Nimbu Ka Achaar

Serves: 6-8

Lemons (*nimbu*), washed, wiped, slit in
quarters without separating the
pieces **2 kg / 4.4 lb**
Juice of lemons **1 kg / 2.2 lb**
Sugar **1 cup / 200 gm / 7 oz**
Black salt (*kala namak*) **250 gm / 9 oz**
Black cardamom (*badi elaichi*) **25 gm**
Black peppercorns (*sabut kali mirch*)
15 gm

Dry red chillies (*sookhi lal mirch*) **25 gm**
Cumin (*jeera*) seeds **2 tbsp / 18 gm**
Black cumin (*shahi jeera*)
seeds **2 tbsp / 20 gm**
Carom (*ajwain*) seeds **2 tbsp / 15 gm**
Asafoetida (*hing*) **a pinch**
Ginger powder (*sonth*) **100 gm / 3½ oz**

Grind the sugar, black salt, black cardamom, black pepper, dry red chillies, cumin seeds, black cumin seeds, carom seeds, asafoetida, and ginger powder together to a fine powder.

Mix ½ cup lemon juice with the powder and stuff the slit lemons with this powder mixture.

Arrange the stuffed lemons in a glass jar, with a layer of the powder mixture between them. Repeat till all the lemons and powder mixture are used up. Pour the remaining lemon juice.

Cover with a thick cloth for the first 2 days and then put the jar out in the sun for 2 weeks, shaking occasionally. This pickle aids digestion and can stay for up to 25 years.

Stuffed Green Chilli Pickle
Hari Mirch Ka Achaar

Serves: 6-8

INGREDIENTS:

Green chillies, long and thick 1 kg / 2.2 lb
For the filling:
Salt 200 gm / 7 oz
Mustard seeds (*rai*), powdered 200 gm / 4½ oz
Turmeric (*haldi*) powder 1½ tsp / 4½ gm
Aniseed (*saunf*), coarsely pounded 1 tbsp / 7½ gm
Onion seeds (*kalonji*) ½ tsp / ¾ gm
Asafoetida (*hing*) a pinch
Lemon (*nimbu*) juice 5

METHOD:

Wash and wipe dry the green chillies. Make a vertical slit in the centre of each chilli.

For the filling, mix all the spices together. Add lemon juice and mix well again.

Fill each chilli with a generous amount of this mixture. Store the stuffed chillies in an opaque jar and keep in the sun for 4-5 days. Shake the jar twice every day.

The chillies will become softer as the days go by, but can be consumed as soon as the filling sticks to the chillies.

Note: *Do not use a glass jar to store this pickle as the green chillies get discoloured.*

Potato Pickle
Aloo Achaar

Serves: 2-4

Potatoes, preferably lemon-sized ones **500 gm / 1.1 lb**
Sesame (*til*) seeds **2 tbsp / 10 gm**
Cumin (*jeera*) seeds **1 tsp / 2 gm**
Salt to taste
Juice of lemons (*nimbu*) **2**
Mustard (*sarson*) oil **4 tbsp / 60 ml / 2 fl oz**
Fenugreek seeds (*methi dana*) ½ tsp / 2¼ gm
Green chillies, split **5 - 6**
Turmeric (*haldi*) powder ½ tsp / 1½ gm
Green coriander (*hara dhaniya*) for garnishing

METHOD:

Boil, peel, and cut the potatoes into halves.

Dry roast the sesame seeds and cumin seeds in a pan. Grind together with a little water.

Transfer the potatoes to a serving dish; add the ground spices, salt, and lemon juice. Mix well.

Heat the oil in a pan; add fenugreek seeds. When they crackle, add green chillies; cook covered for a minute. Add turmeric powder and pour the tempering over the potatoes. Mix well, garnish with green coriander and serve cold.

Raw Papaya Salad
Papita Salad

Serves: 2-4

Papaya (*papita*), raw, small, peeled, coarsely grated **250 gm / 9 oz**
Vegetable oil **1 tsp / 5 ml**
Asafoetida (*hing*) **a pinch**
Mustard seeds (*rai*) **¼ tsp**
Green chillies, slit **4-5**
Cumin (*jeera*) seeds **¼ tsp**
Sugar **1 tsp / 3 gm**
Groundnuts (*moongphalli*), chopped **1 tbsp / 10 gm**
Juice of lemon (*nimbu*) **1**
Green coriander (*hara dhaniya*), finely chopped **1 tsp**
Salt to taste

METHOD:

Heat the oil in a pan; add asafoetida and mustard seeds. When they start spluttering, add green chillies and sauté.

Add the papaya, cumin seeds, sugar, groundnuts, lemon juice, green coriander, and salt; mix thoroughly, and remove from heat. Keep aside to cool.

Serve cold as an accompaniment.

Sprouted Green Gram Salad
Fangevela Mag

Serves: 2-4

INGREDIENTS:

Whole green gram (*moong dal*), soaked for
    8 hours 1⅔ cups / 250 gm / 9 oz
Vegetable oil 1 tsp / 5 ml
Mustard seeds (*rai*) ½ tsp / 1½ gm
Asafoetida (*hing*) ¼ tsp / 1 gm
Water 1 cup / 250 ml / 8 fl oz
Soda bicarbonate ¼ tsp / 1½ gm
Salt to taste
Sugar ½ tsp / 1½ gm
Cumin (*jeera*) powder 1 tsp / 3 gm
Turmeric (*haldi*) powder ¼ tsp
Red chilli powder ¾ tsp / 1½ gm
Coriander (*dhaniya*) powder 1 tsp / 3 gm

METHOD:

Drain the green gram and tie in a muslin cloth. Keep the cloth inside a vessel in a cool place and cover it tightly. Keep aside for 24 hours to allow the green gram to sprout.

Heat the oil in a pan; add mustard seeds. Once they crackle, add asafoetida and sprouted green gram.

Add water, soda bicarbonate, salt, sugar, and the spices. Mix well. Cook covered for 10 minutes or until tender.

Serve hot with any curry and stuffed bread.

INGREDIENTS:

Prawns, small, shelled,
   deveined 1¼ cups / 250 gm / 9 oz
**Grind to a smooth paste with
6 tbsp vinegar:**
Kashmiri chillies (*sookhi lal mirch*)
   10-12
Cumin (*jeera*) seeds 1 tsp / 2 gm
Mustard seeds (*rai*), optional
   ½ tsp / 1½ gm
Black peppercorns (*sabut kali mirch*)
   ½ tsp / 2 gm

Turmeric (*haldi*) powder ½ tsp / 1½ gm
Garlic (*lasan*), chopped 3 tsp / 18 cloves
Ginger (*adrak*), chopped 2 tsp / 2″ piece

Vegetable oil 1 cup / 250 ml / 8 fl oz
Onions, medium-sized, chopped 2
Curry leaves (*kadhi patta*) 8-10
Vinegar (*sirka*) 6 tbsp / 90 ml / 3 fl oz
Green chillies, slit 2
Salt to taste
Sugar 2 tsp / 6 gm

METHOD:

Heat the oil in a pan; sauté onions till soft and golden. Add curry leaves and the ground paste; sauté for 3 minutes, stirring constantly.

Add the prawns and stir-fry for a few minutes.

Add the vinegar, green chillies, salt, and sugar. Cook uncovered for 10 minute Adjust seasoning.

Remove from heat. Bottle when cool. Serve with rice and curry.

Mixed Vegetables in Yoghurt
Mixed Raita

Yoghurt (*dahi*) 2 cups / 500 gm / 1.1 lb
Cumin (*jeera*) seeds 1 tsp / 2 gm
Coriander (*dhaniya*) seeds 1 tsp / 2 gm
Black peppercorns (*sabut kali mirch*) ½ tsp / 2 gm
Salt to taste
Cucumber (*khira*), medium-sized, chopped ½
Green chillies, finely chopped 2
Mint (*pudina*) leaves, finely chopped 1 tsp / 2 gm
Onions, chopped 3 tbsp / 36 gm / 1¼ oz
Tomatoes, chopped 30 gm / 1 oz
Red chilli powder a pinch

METHOD:

Heat a griddle (tawa) and broil the cumin seeds, coriander seeds, and black peppercorns till dark and aromatic. Pound and keep aside.

Whisk the yoghurt with salt. Add all the vegetables.

Pour into a glazed earthenware bowl. Sprinkle some red chilli powder and the pounded spices.

Serve chilled.

Variation: *60 gm / 2 oz squeezed pineapple chunks can also be added.*

Crisp Gram Flour Granules in Yoghurt
Boondi Raita

Serves: 4

INGREDIENTS:

Gram flour (*besan*) **2½ tbsp / 25 gm**
Salt **¼ tsp**
Baking powder **½ tsp / 2 gm**
Water as required
Vegetable oil for frying
Yoghurt (*dahi*), thick **4 cups / 1 lt / 32 oz**
Cumin (*jeera*) seeds, roasted, crushed **a pinch**
Red chilli powder **½ tsp / 1½ gm**

METHOD:

Mix the gram flour, salt, and baking powder in a bowl. Whisk into a smooth batter with a little water.

Heat the oil in a pan; pour about 2 tbsp batter, at a time, through a slotted spoon to form small granules. These will froth in the hot oil, then rise to the surface. Fry until crisp and golden. Remove and drain the excess oil. Repeat till all the batter is used up.

Transfer the gram flour granules in a bowl containing warm water. When the granules turn soft, squeeze the excess water. Keep aside.

Whisk the yoghurt with salt, cumin seeds, red chilli powder in a bowl until smooth and creamy.

Add the gram flour granules and serve at room temperature or chilled.

Index

BREADS

ACCOMPANIMENTS